Professional Diploma in

GW00888859

Examined unit:

Delivering Customer Value Through Marketing

First edition 2009, Second edition 2012

ISBN 9781 4453 9159 5

e ISBN 9781 4453 9628 6

British Library Cataloguing-in-Publication Data
A catalogue record for this book is available from the British Library

Published by

BPP Learning Media Ltd,
BPP House, Aldine Place,
142-144 Uxbridge Road,
London W12 8AA

www.bpp.com/learningmedia

Printed in the United Kingdom by Ricoh

Ricoh House
Ullswater Crescent
Coulsdon
CR5 2HR

We are grateful to the Chartered Institute of Marketing for permission to reproduce material.

Welcome to BPP Learning Media's **Professional Diploma in Marketing passcards**, covering the examined unit: **Delivering Customer Value Through Marketing**

Passcards help you prepare for exams.

- They **focus on your exam** and **save you time**.
- They incorporate **diagrams** to kick start your memory.
- They follow the overall **structure** of the BPP Learning Media Study Text, but BPP Learning Media's CIM **Passcards** are not just a condensed book. Each card has been separately designed for clear presentation. Topics are self contained and can be grasped visually.
- CIM **Passcards** are still **just the right size** for pockets, briefcases and bags.

Run through the **Passcards** as often as you can during your final revision period. The day before the exam, try to go through the **Passcards** again! You will then be well on your way to passing your exams.

Good luck!

Contents

		Page
1	New product development and positioning	1
2	Developing the product portfolio	11
3	Branding and branding strategies	21
4	Pricing, concepts & setting	29
5	Channel management	39
6	Intermediaries and stakeholders	55
7	Contracts & SLAs	67

		Page
8	Managing marketing communications	75
9	MarComms activities and measurement	91
10	Managing agency relationships	99
11	Customer service and care	113
12	Managing key accounts	127
13	Sales/product information & relationship risks	135
14	Analysing the case material/preparing for the exam	143

1: New product development and positioning

Topic List

What is a product?

NPD: adoption & innovation

Standardisation

Product positioning

Products and services are the lifeblood of any organisation as they not only generate revenues and therefore ultimately profits for the organisation, they also create value for the customer. This section explores the components of a product, the process for developing new products, the importance of product positioning and the concept of product adoption.

The **core product** comprises the functionality and key benefits of the product.

The **actual product** comprises a range of 'add-ons' beyond the core product and offers potential for differentiation, eg product features, packaging and design.

The **augmented (or extended) product** comprises potential customer value beyond the core and actual product elements, eg after sales service, guarantee, delivery and returns policy.

Kotler *et al* (2008, p500) define a product as 'anything that is offered to the market for attention, acquisition, use or consumption that might satisfy a need or want. Products include more than just tangible goods'. They go on to define a service as 'products that consist of activities, benefits, or satisfactions that are offered for sale that are essentially intangible and do not result in the ownership of anything'.

A product can be a physical good, service, idea or indeed, a publicist might treat a celebrity as a brand.

Product levels

Product levels

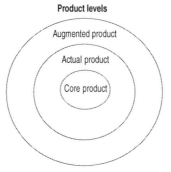

Augmented product

Actual product

Core product

Summary of product levels

The core product	This is the basic product ie, what the customer is buying. Marketers must define the core product elements in terms that are meaningful to the customer.
The actual product	It is composed of several characteristics such as styling, brand, quality, and packaging.
The augmented product	Additional customer benefits and services are added. This could include things like warranties, guarantees, finance terms, or a dedicated helpline.

Consumer products versus industrial products

Consumer products	Industrial products
Convenience products	Raw materials
Shopping products	Major equipment
Speciality products	Accessory equipment
Unsought products	Component parts/ Process materials/ Consumer supplies/ Industrial services

NPD: the new product development process comprises a number of recognised stages which enable an organisation to apply a structured approach to generating and evaluating ideas and deciding which ones to take through development and onto launch.

Developing new products

NPD: reduces the possibility of product obsolescence, so that a range of products to meet customer needs will always be available

- Ensures the product range continues to remain relevant in the light of changes in the organisation's external environment
- Enables the organisation to compete in new and developing markets
- Can reduce the dependence on vulnerable product sectors; a range of products can weather changing economic conditions
- Can achieve long-term growth and profit by ensuring a better fit with customer needs and expectations
- Responds to changing customer needs and expectations

The recognised stages in the NPD process

New production acceptance innovation/diffusion model

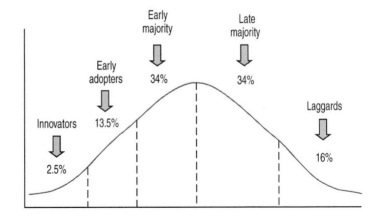

Idea generation: ideas should be generated from as many sources as possible, both internally and externally. Ideas might come from staff, particularly those in customer-facing roles. Customers are also an excellent source of ideas for new and enhanced products.

Screening: this is the process of evaluating all of the ideas that have been generated. It is necessary as not all of the ideas will be suitable, feasible and acceptable to the organisation. Criteria should be used in order to decide which ideas should progress to concept testing.

Types of new product

Brassington and Pettitt (2006) suggest that there are broadly four types:

- New to company and market:
- New to company, significant innovation for market:
- New to company, minor innovation for market
- New to company, no innovation for market

Product standardisation: this is a decision for an organisation that is entering a new market, especially internationally. With standardisation the same product and often the same marketing mix, is used with both the existing and new market.

Production adaptation: often, when an organisation, enters a new market, especially internationally, the process involves tailoring the product, and often the entire marketing mix, to meet the specific needs of the local market.

Strategy	Summary of strategy
Keep product the same worldwide (standardisation)	The product is the same worldwide, ie, there is no product development required.
Adapt the product for each market (adaptation)	The product is changed for each market to meet local needs.
Develop a new product	Create a new product for each overseas market.

Product positioning

Positioning is 'arranging for a product to occupy a clear, distinctive and desirable place relative to competing products in the minds of target consumers' (Kotler *et al*, 2008, p157). This means the product must be clearly positioned against the competition and must have a distinct image in the market.

Kotler *et al* (2008, p432) say that 'products are created in the factory, but brands are created in the mind'. Clearly, positioning has a key role to play in achieving this.

Perceived position mapped against quality and price

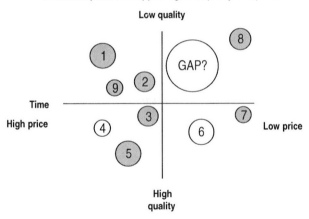

Number of Adaptation

2: Developing the product portfolio

Topic List

Product management

Customer value

Product portfolio management

This section deals with the advantages of strategic product management and, at the same time, considers the limitations and how these might be managed. There are a variety of different techniques including the PLC (product life cycle), the BCG matrix, and the GE matrix. These offer a number of options to achieve effective product management and will be set in various contexts.

Product management: the organisational function that has ultimate responsibility for the product range. Key goals will include growing income and profit from the portfolio and ensuring that the organisation's products align with the marketing environment.

Product management focus

In today's environment, product managers are most likely to be focused on a number or priority areas:

- Increasing product profitability
- Generating new revenue streams
- Delivering and supporting products in a cost-effective way
- Retaining existing (valuable) customers
- Cross-selling and up-selling to existing customers
- New customer acquisition

Marketing mix	Commentary
Product	The right product(s) available to meet current customer needs (added value). The product range can be expanded or collapsed as needs change.
Price	It is important to understand how customers perceive price, so the organisation must be clear on exactly how to price its products and the relationship with any other products within its portfolio.
Promotion	A range of tools is available to support the product, create customer satisfaction and loyalty through careful positioning in the customer's mind. Branding reinforces the product image with the consumer.
Place	It is necessary to get the products to customers where they want to purchase not where you would like them to purchase.
Physical evidence	Where services are concerned, some tangibility needs to be provided to support the overall proposition. This could range from brochures to the decor of the office where the service is delivered.
People	Arguably the most important element, who need to be consistent and professional and reflect the brand.
Processes	It is important to train staff and have defined processes in place to support staff in delivering a consistent and a high quality service.

Customer needs (Blythe, 2006)

Needs	Summary
Current product need	Identified through research, are the key features and benefits of the product acceptable or do they need to be enhanced?
Future needs	Identifying future demand levels and product functionality is difficult, but effective management of the product life cycle supported by ongoing research will assist.
Pricing levels	While customers may want to buy at the 'best' price, this is often based on quality v cost issues and the balance must be understood.
Information needs	What information does the customer need to commit to the purchase? How can this information be conveyed?
Product availability	Customers generally want the product available to them in a readily accessible way and therefore the choice of distribution channel and channel's members is crucial.

Customer value: the total of the benefits a customer receives, as a result of buying products or services from the organisation, and the customer's overall experience of the organisation's customer service offering. This will have a significant impact on the organisation's ability to retain customers and to build customer loyalty.

Customer value is derived from a customer-centric organisation that understands its customers. The better it understands them, the better value achieved through the deployment of the marketing mix. Customers define value, not the organisation and organisations must stay close to the dynamic nature of this definition in order to keep the product portfolio relevant to customer needs.

Value is derived either directly or indirectly through better customer services, brand reputation, market coverage and technology, pricing or cost savings.

Product life cycle (PLC): this concept is based on the principle that once products are developed and launched they will all, broadly, follow a similar pattern of demand that flows through growth, maturity and then onto decline.

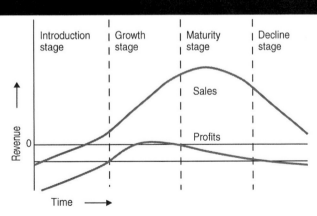

The role of the marketing mix throughout the PLC

Marketing mix	Introduction	Growth	Maturity	Decline
Product	Basic product, but quality assured and any legal protection needed is in place	Additional product features may be added or existing features enhanced	More variety	Maintain, harvest or discontinue
Price	Skim or penetrate the market	Maintain	Maybe lowered to match or beat the competition	Maintain
Place	Selective or limited	Increasing in line with demand	Now reaching critical mass	Now declining
Promotion	Build awareness or tell people how to use the product. Often high impact/awareness	Broader audience which may be for building image or encouraging repeat purchase	Now about reminding and encouraging purchase	Reminding may also be confirming discontinuation

2: Developing the product portfolio

Boston Consulting Group (BCG) matrix: a widely used product management tool which enables the product manager to track the performance of the entire product portfolio. Products are categorised based on relative market share and market growth. The BCG matrix categorises products as "dogs, stars, cash cows" or "problem children" (also known as "question marks").

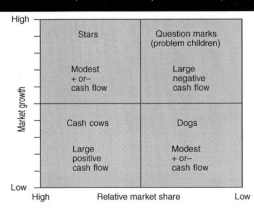

The BCG matrix can operate at a number of levels including:

- Corporate
- Product
- SBU (Strategic Business Unit)

Product strategies

There are four main strategies that product managers should consider using for products within the BCG categories and at different stages in their life cycle:

1 **Build:** invest (in marketing activities) in an attempt to increase market share, eg to move a problem child product into the star category.

2 **Hold:** here the product manager will invest just enough in order to keep the product in its present category, eg to maintain a cash cow.

3 **Harvest:** reduce the amount of investment in order to maximise the short-term cash flows and profits from the product

4 **Divest/withdraw:** investment is no longer justified and the decision is taken to 'wind down' support for the product, with a view to withdrawing it from the market altogether, eg typically used for dogs.

General Electric (GE) matrix: a useful product management tool, which is often used alongside the BCG matrix. The GE matrix enables the products to be categorised based on industry attractiveness and business strengths.

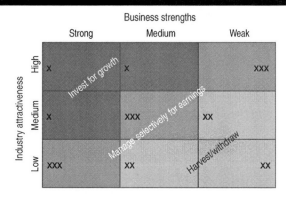

3: Branding and branding strategies

Topic List

Branding categories

Building a brand

Branding strategies

Global branding

There is probably as much written about brands, branding and brand management as there is about all of the other marketing activities combined. In the eyes of the target audience the brand 'is' the organisation. Unlike other areas of marketing, which are often effectively processes and where frameworks exist, branding is much more about emotion. Brands with powerful and positive images are highly valuable. However, brands which are perceived negatively can have a very serious (negative) impact on the organisation's success.

Brand: a name, term, sign, symbol or design which has been created in order that customers can identify the product in the market and differentiate it from other products in the market.

Blythe (2006, p89) defines branding as 'the culmination of a range of activities across the whole marketing mix leading to a brand image that conveys a whole set of messages to the consumer about quality, price, expected performance and status'.

Three types of brands

Three types of brands Dibb *et al* (2005) suggest three types of brand:

- Manufacturer (corporate brand)
- Own-label
- Generic

Brand management: marketing activities which aim to both protect and grow the brand and, ultimately, lead to the organisation achieving its desired positioning for the brand. Typically, this will involve monitoring changes in the organisation's marketing environment, especially competitor brands, and deploying an appropriate communications mix to support the brand.

Successful brands (based on De Pelsmacker *et al*, 2004)

Building a brand (De Pelsmacker *et al*, 2004) means that an organisation will invest significant sums of money building a brand's favourable image and position in the marketplace, such that long term benefits will be achieved both in brand awareness (recognition) and brand value (financial).

Brand values: an effective brand depicts the philosophy and beliefs of the organisation, which are reflected, to the consumer, through the values portrayed within the brand and how it is positioned. Examples of values are quality, reliability, innovation, fun, safety and value for money.

Brand equity: the actual asset value placed on the brand itself. It is notoriously difficult to value, unlike physical assets. Brand equity will be strongly influenced by the level of awareness of the brand and how it is perceived within the market.

Brand value is established through emotional connectivity with the customer, with the brand itself reinforcing, to the customer, reassurance and creditability while also portraying the specific brand attributes.

Four possible strategies for brands

1 Brand stretching

Stretch the brand (brand extension) typically into a new or modified product in a similar category.

2 Line extension

Here the organisation develops a new product closely related to an existing product by developing a new form. This is quite common as it is a low-cost and generally low-risk.

3 Multi branding

Organisations often introduce additional brands within the same category.

4 New brands

Sometimes an existing brand will not fit in a new product category. The choice of branding strategy depends on what the organisation is trying to achieve.

3: Branding and branding strategies

Rebranding: where an existing brand in the market is either adapted or changed completely. This can be an expensive exercise and might be undertaken simply to 'rejuvenate' the brand, or to appeal to a new/wider audience. It may happen where the original brand is perceived negatively or where a merger or acquisition has taken place.

Sometimes it is necessary to reposition a product in the mind of the consumer and this can be for a variety of reasons ranging from price differentiation to expanding into overseas markets. It can be done to overcome perceived service problems, or position the product more correctly in the consumer's mind.

Arguments in favour of global brands (Yeshin, 2006) are:

- Economies of scale through standardisation across each market
- Developing technology ensures similar product use
- Rapid and readily available communication channels such as the internet and satellite TV
- Increasing similarity between segments across countries
- Global brands can be seen as better quality than local brands

4: Pricing, concepts & setting

Topic List

The role of pricing in product management

Pricing frameworks

Pricing in international markets

Perceived product value

You will need to deepen your understanding of the impact that a variety of pricing strategies can have on the product position in the market. Pricing can be used to manage the product at various stages in its life cycle in order to maximise the appeal of the product and profitability.

Setting pricing objectives as a benchmark and to guide strategic product development is an important part of marketing.

According to Doyle (2000, p116) price is 'the amount of money that customers pay for the product. It includes discounts, allowances and credit terms'. Price is the value that someone is prepared to pay for the product or service. It is also the one element of the marketing mix that generates revenue, income and profit for the organisation, ie, it has a direct impact on the bottom line and needs careful management.

Setting prices is a strategic decision that must be reflected in the other elements of the marketing mix. Potential consumers will have a perception about price in relation to the organisation's promotion style, including the brand, the product itself and where it can be purchased.

There are six key factors summarised in the table below to consider when making pricing decisions:

1. **Pricing objectives:** What are the pricing objectives to support the business objectives?

2. **Buyers' perception:** What does the price mean to the customer?

3. **Perceived value for money:** What benefit will the customer receive from the product?

4. **The competition:** How are competitors pricing their products?

5. **Marketing mix:** Does our pricing reflect the other elements of the marketing mix?

6. **Channel members:** What are the implications of price for the distribution channel?

Pricing objectives (based on Dibb *et al*, 2005)

Pricing objective	Summary
Survival	Here the organisation simply wants to ensure it remains in business.
Profit	Organisations generally like to increase profits on a year-on-year basis. Therefore taking into account potential sales a specific profit level will be anticipated.
Market share	Here it is the share of market that is important (ie market leader) and therefore an organisation will be willing to reduce price(s) to maintain its market position.
Cash flow	Cash generation is very important in some organisations and the price is set to bring cash into the organisation quickly.
Status quo	An organisation may simply want to retain its position in the market compared with the competition, ie be content to be the 'number 2' in a particular category and therefore while it may match the price offered by the competition it has no intention of beating them on price.
Product quality	Here the organisation wants to offer the 'best product' in terms of quality. In terms of the price paid it could be considerably be more expensive than similar products. However, if reliability is more important to the purchaser because breakdowns mean lost income, which potentially would be well in excess of any quality premium, then a high price can be justified.

Value for money

This is the benefit the customer derives from the purchase of the product. The organisation needs to understand the value that the customer places on the benefits received and then price the product accordingly. Effectively, customers assess the price and measure the benefits received. The benefits can be measurable and real or associated with confidence, or status.

Other factors which affect the perceived value of the product include:

- Service and after-sales service quality

- Level of differentiation from competitor products

- Quality of any packaging

- Product functionality

- Any substitute products which may be available

Skimming: a pricing strategy for new products where the product has a clear advantage in the market at the time of launch and therefore a high launch price can be achieved.

Mark-up: profit expressed as a percentage of the production and other costs of an item.

Profit margin: profit expressed as a percentage of the selling price of an item.

Pricing strategies

Pricing strategies	Summary
Cost based	Includes cost plus and mark-up pricing and breakeven analysis
Customer based	This includes: psychological pricing, differential, product-line and promotional pricing
Competitor based	Pricing near or away from the competition
Professional pricing	The price does not relate to the time taken providing the service

Price elasticity of demand: the relationship between price and demand. Where demand is 'elastic' even a small change in price might have a dramatic impact on demand. However, where demand is 'inelastic' the product is relatively insensitive to changes in price

There are three forms of elasticity of demand:

- Products are said to have elastic demand where a small increase in price produces a large percentage decrease in demand.
- **Inelastic demand** is where a change in price causes a very small change in demand (or none at all).
- **Unitary demand** is where the percentage change in price results in an identical change in the demand.

Pricing for international markets

Factors which need to be taken into consideration when setting different prices for each market include:

External

- Economic conditions, which may allow a greater (or lower) price to be charged
- Level and strength of competition in each market
- Currency exchange rates operating between markets
- Legal implications, ie selling below cost price on the overseas market

Internal

- Marketing objectives for each market
- Customer perceptions of your brand
- Products position within the PLC

Perceived product value

Beamish and Ashford (2008) suggest the perceived value of a product has a major impact upon the customer's decision to buy. Key factors that affect perceived value include:

- Life cycle of the product: customers will generally be happy to pay extra for 'new' products but will expect to pay less as the product moves through the PLC.
- Service and technical support: should a product break-down, then the availability of 'experts' will be an important consideration.
- Prestige and status are key factors. The purchase of a prestigious brand does not always offer better quality, but it will confer confidence and status to the user.
- Packaging which reflects the status of the product: eg consider the difference in packaging between Sainsbury's 'taste the difference' range and 'basics'range

5: Channel management

Topic List

Channels & strategy

Overseas distribution

Managing relationships

Role of communications

Evaluating options

This section considers the 'place' element of the marketing mix. This focuses on how products are distributed to customers. Channel management, as 'place' is more widely known, is arguably one of the aspects of business which has altered the most in recent years, driven by technological change, the need for greater efficiency and demands from customers for greater choice, flexibility and convenience.

Distribution channel: the means through which the organisation delivers its products and services to the end customer.

Channels of distribution

- Distribution channels refer to a group of individuals or organisations (intermediaries) that move goods from the producer to the consumer or industrial user of the product. In other words a distribution channel is the way an organisation gets its product to the consumer. Sometimes distribution channels are referred to as marketing channels.

- Distribution channels do not just involve physical products, but can equally apply to services which tend to have a shorter channel. Channels can extend beyond geographical boundaries and have an important role to play in overseas markets.

- Without an effective distribution channel, products, even the best products, are more likely to fail, so organisations are continually looking to develop cheaper and faster ways of selling their products.

Supply chain

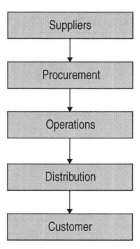

Functions of a distribution channel

Creating utility

Facilitating exchange efficiencies

Alleviating discrepancies

Standardising transactions

Providing Customer service

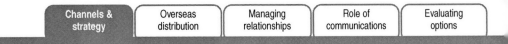

Typical channel structures for business-to-business channels

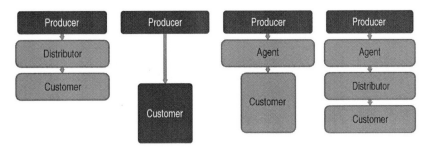

Typical channel structure for B2C market

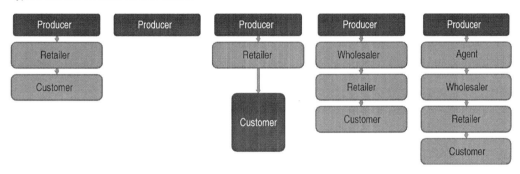

Hotel to customer through many intermediaries

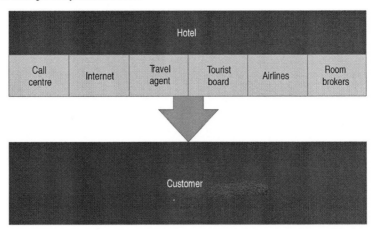

Hotel					
Call centre	Internet	Travel agent	Tourist board	Airlines	Room brokers

Customer

Exclusive distribution: the organisation has very few outlets, reinforcing the exclusive nature of the brand.

Selective distribution: there is a relatively small number of outlets; generally associated with 'premium' brands.

Intensive distribution: products are available on a widespread basis from many different outlets.

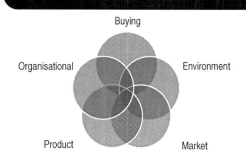

The actual choice of channel or channels can be influenced by five factors (Brassington and Pettitt, 2007): the product, organisational objectives, market size and location, consumer behaviour, changing environment

Marketing channel

Vertical Marketing System (VMS)

In a conventional channel, as identified, roles and responsibilities can be confused, or blurred

Conventional channel

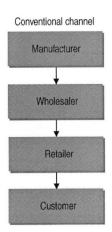

Vertical system

International Channels

An organisation that wants to enter an overseas market must consider the most appropriate entry method. They include:

- A saturated domestic market, where sales are slowing down and the competition is becoming stronger.

- Efficiencies of scale, where the opening of an overseas market reduces the unit cost of production

- Existing customers may be expanding overseas and there is an opportunity to support them.

Six considerations for overseas markets

Paliwoda (1993) suggests six factors to be taken into account:

1 **Speed:** How quickly does the organisation want to enter the market and what share will it obtain in the timescale?

2 **Cost:** What are the costs of the entry methods and which represent better value?

3 **Flexibility:** How much flexibility is needed? ie what are the alternatives if things do not proceed to plan?

4 **Risk:** What is the organisation's view on risk, including financial, reputation, economic and social?

5 **Payback:** How quickly does the investment need to generate a profit, or what level of profit is needed by a certain date in time?

6 **Long term profit objectives:** What are the long term plans for the market?

Overseas options

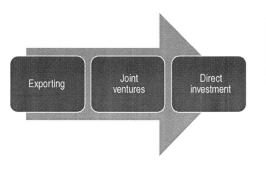

Exporting · Joint ventures · Direct investment

Cateora's 5Cs: coverage, character, continuity, control and cost. A useful framework for the evaluation of options in channel management and the performance of channel partners.

Cateora's Framework

Cateora (1993) offers a framework for evaluation based on 5 Cs that are applicable to both the domestic and international markets.

- **Coverage:** How well the channel performs in achieving sales, or market share, or penetration of the market.

- **Character:** Compatibility of the channel with the organisation's desired positioning for the product.

- **Continuity:** How loyal the various channel members are and the length of time they have been a part of the channel.

- **Control:** How well the organisation is able to control the marketing programmes within the channel; this can be of particular concern where long international channels are involved.

- **Cost:** This will cover the cost of investment, variable costs, and expenditure.

MarComms for Channels

Marketing communications will need to convey not just product information, but relationship building through trust and commitment. This is best done using the DRIP model:

- **Differentiation:** messages explaining how the organisation is different from others in the industry and the competitive advantages it confers.

- **Reminding:** reminding, or reinforcing the importance of the relationship and benefits that the parties accrue from each other as a result of being part of the channel.

- **Informing:** sharing with others exactly what the capabilities of the organisation are. Common or potential areas for misunderstanding can be dealt with in a proactive manner.

- **Persuading:** messages to encourage potential channel members, or encouraging existing members to continue with the relationship.

Evaluation of options

An organisation will evaluate a number of channels and select one or multiple channels that will best meet its business objectives. When selecting the 'best' channel the organisation could use the following three criteria (Kotler *et al*, 1999).

Economic

An estimate of the potential sales, investment and channel costs will be made for each channel. Also, a consideration of any assets that may need to be shared

Control

In order to widen distribution of the product and made it more accessible to customers, intermediaries are used which dilute the overall control.

Adaptive

Establishing a channel usually involves a long-term commitment which goes beyond financial dimensions and the channel needs to be able to respond to changes in the market.

Adoption criteria for new channel partners

- Does the organisation meet the requirements of the chosen channel strategy?

- The experience of the organisation with the particular product / sector.

- The organisation's reputation.

- The 'reach' of the organisation, ie can sufficient customers access products via the organisation?

- Is there a 'fit' between the two organisations? Are they culturally-aligned and share common goals?

- Can acceptable pricing be agreed?

- Is it possible to agree terms and conditions?

- Can the organisation deliver to the required service standards?

- Does the organisation deal with competitors (a potential conflict of interest)?

- Can we do business with them (possible to interact with them on a personal level)?

6: Intermediaries and stakeholders

Topic List

Intermediaries

Stakeholders in channel management

Dealing with conflict in the channel

Communicating with stakeholders

Having examined the different types of channel strategies, we will now consider the various intermediaries which are most commonly found within channel structures. In this section we will also consider the importance and role of the broader stakeholder community.

Intermediaries and descriptions of their roles

Type of intermediary	Description
Wholesalers	■ **Merchant wholesalers**: independently owned businesses that take title to the goods and include full-service and limited service wholesalers (see below) ■ **Full service wholesalers**: these wholesalers offer services such as maintaining stock levels. ■ **Limited service wholesalers**: as the name implies they offer a reduced level of services and include: cash-and-carry and mail order wholesalers.
Retailers	Consumer-facing and will have purchased the products from the wholesaler (above) or direct from the manufacturer. Retailers take ownership and physical possession and sell direct to the consumer.
Distributors/dealers	Distributors have the right to sell the products in a defined geographical area and can add value to the product by making it available locally to the consumer. Dealers add value by offering their expertise as well as representing the manufacturer.
Franchisees	The most common franchise allows the franchisee (the person or business who has the contract) to sell a specific product or service in accordance with the agreed terms .
Licensee	Similar to a franchise, but not as comprehensive. Typically the licensee is given the right to operate a business for a particular organisation within a given area.

Type of intermediary	Description
Agents/brokers	This group of intermediaries will act on behalf of the organisation, but will not take ownership or legal title to the product.
	■ **Brokers**: Their role is primarily to bring the buyer together with the seller.
	■ **Agents**: There are four types of agent:
	– Manufacturers' agent: sell similar lines from more than one manufacturer.
	– Selling agent: has the ability to sell a manufacturer's entire range.
	– Purchasing agent: buy goods, receive them and inspect them for quality.
	– Commission merchants: possession of the goods is obtained, with payment by way of commission.

Three groups of value-added service provided by intermediaries (based on Webster, 1979)

Element	Description
Information	Collection and distribution of market research and intelligence data, such as sales data to help the planning process.
Management	Setting objectives and channel plans along with any risk that needs to be taken or managed.
Matching	Adjusting the offer to fit a buyer's needs, including grading, assembling and packaging.
Promotion	Setting promotional objectives and communicating through the different tools.
Price	Setting pricing policies and financing policies.
Distribution	Managing the transport, storing and stock control of goods.
Customer service	Providing channels for advice support and after sales service.
Relationships	Facilitating communication and maintaining relationships in the channel.

Intermediaries' impact on profitability

- **Increased sales**: the intermediary can have its own sales team with an expert knowledge of the domestic and overseas markets

- As the intermediary will often take ownership of the goods, it will also **take responsibility for taking stock away from the manufacturer.**

- **Packaging together** of groups of products to widen customer choice/appeal

- **Efficiency**: rather than dealing with possibly hundreds of retailers, distribution and hence control can be managed through a few wholesalers

- **Warehousing and transport costs can be shared** with other organisations, which may also eliminate the need for purpose-built facilities

- The value added by the intermediary may allow the price of the product to be **premium priced.**

Stakeholder: any individual, group, organisation or body which is might affect or be affected by an organisation's decisions and/or activities.

Stakeholders

Stakeholders can comprise many different individuals, groups, organisations and bodies. To be classified as an organisation's stakeholder the individual, group, organisation or body must affect or be affected by an organisation's decisions and/or activities. Essentially, a stakeholder is anyone with an interest in the organisation and/or its activities.Channel members are **connected stakeholders**, ie they have an economic or contractual relationship with the organisation.Fill (2006) suggests that there are two main concerns when moving a product through the distribution channel:

- Management of the product (supply chain)

- Management of the intangible aspects of ownership and the communication between the different stakeholders

The six markets framework highlights the key stakeholder markets

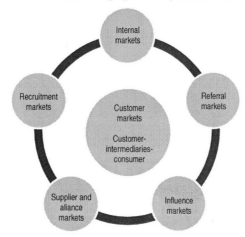

Mendelow's stakeholder power/interest matrix

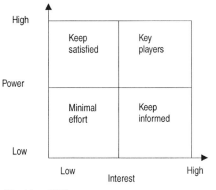

(Mendelow, 1991)

Mendelow (1991) developed the concept of stakeholder mapping based on stakeholder power/interest, enabling an organisation's management to identify and categorise the organisation's key stakeholders. The matrix enables the organisation to prioritise and allocate appropriate resources to stakeholder management and to develop appropriate communications and relationship management strategies for each stakeholder group.

Power dependency

Some members will have significant influence over members; this can be termed power dependency. Power dependency can manifest itself in a number of ways;

- **Reward power**: where one channel member has the ability to reward another member

- **Coercive power**: rather than rewarding a channel member, a form of penalty could be imposed

- **Expert power**: where the member is seen as having some specialist knowledge not easily replaceable

Underlying conflict areas

Areas of conflict	Summary
Incompatible goals	Members of the channel disagree on a range of issues, including strategy, new ways of doing things, or financial returns.
Role conflict	Members of the channel cannot agree on the role each should take.
Domain differences	This concerns which organisation should make the marketing decisions
Perceptions of reality	Different channel members may interpret issues in different ways
Expectations	Changed circumstances may bring about a change in the way channel members want to do things in the future.

Communication with channels

The responsibility for communication must rest with the channel leader or a nominated party. The communication consists of two components:

- **Data flows**: the operational, ie day-to-day, information that flows across the channel.

- **Marketing communications**: the use of the promotional mix designed to influence the channel to take a particular course of action. Other purposes include motivation, goodwill and understanding.

The data flows between organisations can extend beyond operational and cover market and strategic data flows. Communication needs to be consistent and co-ordinated to ensure the shared values and attitudes of the various stakeholders are maintained.

7: Contracts & SLAs

Topic List

The legal framework

Service level agreements (SLAs)

Measuring the effectiveness of intermediaries

Monitoring performance

Organisations need to be reassured that the investments made in developing customer-focused channels will be rewarded through satisfied customers and the prospect of an acceptable return on their money.

While many organisations may have worked together for many years and 'trust' has been the foundation of the relationship, increasingly organisations are formalising their relationships through contracts and service level agreements. This ensures that when things do go wrong, each of the parties to the agreement can adopt a specific course of action to correct the situation. Of course, if the contracts are well written the consequences will have been anticipated and action taken proactively to address the issues.

Legal framework

The legal framework that applies to marketing will cover aspects such as contract law, protection for consumers, finance, competition and trading practice.

In the UK, parliament is responsible for passing legislation, but, increasingly, implementation is the responsibility of other bodies such as the Office of Fair Trading (OFT). In Europe, there is an approach to standardise legalisation across member states and for some organisations, this will be welcome news.

Legislation is most profound in the area of competition and varies according to the local laws, customs and practices in different countries. In the international economy, there is no one legal system and the organisation that uses different channels in different countries will in effect be responsible for adhering to the laws of each of the countries in which it operates.

Common law has guided legal systems in most countries of the world, requiring disputes to be solved on the basis of tradition, common practice and the interpretation of existing statutes.

Civil law, on the other hand, has at its basis that all foreseeable circumstances are identified and codes of law are then written for the various legal sectors such as commercial, civil or common applications. This includes issues such as copying, the use of brand names, and impact on the nature and profitability of international trade

Contractual requirements

A range of contractual issues are identified below.

Restricted sales area

A producer will often grant a specific geographical area (postcode area, town, or region) to an intermediary such as an agent or distributor.

Tying contract

In return for the rights to sell a particular product, producers may insist that intermediaries must purchase other items as well.

Exclusive deal

A producer may insist that an intermediary does not stock competitor products, ie offers an exclusive deal only.

Refusal to deal

Producers, as we have seen earlier, go to considerable trouble to select the right distributor for their products. Equally, they may choose not to allow certain intermediaries to distribute their products for a variety of reasons.

The specification

A specification is a clear statement or description of what the buyer wants the supplier to perform, including where it is to be carried out and/or delivered, when and to what quality or other standard. It is an essential component of contractual relationships.

SLAs

A service level agreement (SLA) sets outs the minimum level of service a third party can expect to receive measured against set dimensions.

The SLA has three main objectives, which are to:

- Act as a point of differentiation
- Improve quality
- Improve customer service

Organisations, particularly those offering some form of service, are generally considered to be similar (eg financial service providers), so establishing some form of differentiation can be seen as a competitive advantage.

The SLA is usually written or published on the organisation's website and should:

- Clearly establish the organisation's needs
- Simplify complex issues so that they are clearly understood by both parties
- Reduce areas of conflict by identifying them at the outset of the relationship

Measuring effectiveness

Typical criteria for measuring the effectiveness of intermediaries include:

- Sales: target levels of sales to be achieved in a given period

- Stock levels: minimum levels of stock which must be maintained

- Delivery times: maximum time between order and delivery

- Returns policy: maximum period in which faulty goods can be returned

- Training programmes: minimum number of staff to be trained in a set period

- Customer service: maximum time a telephone call can go unanswered, complaint handling times

- Customer retention rates.

Key Performance Indicator (KPI): used in performance management and measurement. KPIs are focused on significant goals and are useful in ensuring that the organisation remains on course to achieve its key objectives.

Balanced Scorecard (BSC): used in performance management and measurement. The BBS focuses on a number of key areas (typically four quadrants) where achievement of objectives is important if the organisation is to achieve against its higher level goals.

Balanced Scorecard

Devised by Kaplan and Norton (1992), the BSC is a commonly used tool in performance management. Typically focusing on four quadrants (often financial, customers, processes and innovation), but there could be more, it enables the organisation to identify a number of key areas of importance and to base performance targets on these.

Monitoring Performance

Performance against SLAs and other targets can be monitored in a number of ways, including:

- Complaints tracking
- Observation
- Mystery shopping
- Spot checks
- Sample checking
- Customer research/feedback
- Self-assessment by the service provider

8: Managing marketing communications

Topic List

Marketing communications planning

MarComms in CRM

Internal MarComms

External audiences

In this section, we consider the relevance of marketing communications in the organisation and how marketing communications objectives must align to the organisation's corporate goals. The marketing communications plan is an extremely important topic, as is a consideration of the different strategies for marketing communications.

Marketing communications (MarComms): another term for 'promotion', which is an element of the marketing mix. Marketing communications involves a range of activities with the purpose of conveying marketing messages to target audiences.

'Marketing communications is a management process through which an organisation engages with its various audiences'. By understanding an audience's communication environment, organisations seek to develop and present messages for its identified stakeholder groups, before evaluating and acting upon the responses. By conveying messages that are of significant value, audiences are encouraged to offer attitudinal and behavioural responses'. Fill (2006, p2)

Pickton and Broderick (2005, p4) provide the following definition: 'All the promotional elements of the marketing mix which involve the communications between an organisation and its target audiences on all matters that affect marketing performance'.

DRIP

Fill (2002, p48) defines the role of marketing communications as either to:

- **Differentiate**: to make a product or brand appear to be different to that of a competitor.

- **Remind**: to reassure the target audience as to the benefits of making a purchase.

- **Inform**: to provide new information to a target audience, for example about a new product.

- **Persuade**: to encourage a target audience towards an action or to change an opinion.

Marketing communications is essential to achieve positioning and to portray brand value to the target audience. It can also be used to build loyalty and to support customer retention, as well as supporting new business acquisition activities.

MarComms Objectives

The communications objectives are directly derived from the marketing objectives that in turn come from the corporate objectives, themselves coming from the organisation's mission statement.

A typical hierarchy could look like that shown

- Organisational mission statement

- Corporate objectives

- Functional objectives (which will include mentioning objectives)

- Marketing communication objectives

Hierarchy of objectives

Marketing communications plan: a structured and considered framework for analysing an organisation's current situation, identifying and analysing target audiences and designing specific messages for them delivered through execution of an appropriately tailored communications mix. An effective plan should also include budget considerations and proposals for measurement.

Framework for a marketing communications plan

1 Situation/context analysis
2 Set communications objectives
3 Target market profile
4 Marketing communications strategy (push/pull/profile)
5 Segmentation, targeting and positioning
6 Develop the communications message
7 Develop an integrated communications mix
8 Schedule media
9 Set promotional budget
10 Allocate resources
11 Execute and monitor
12 Evaluate effectiveness

Typical marketing communications objectives might focus on:

- Changing perception
- Creating/building awareness
- Achieving positioning (or re-positioning)
- Influencing the target audience
- Generating sales (volumes and/or revenues)
- Improving customer retention
- Improving customer satisfaction
- Supporting the launch of a new product

The importance of setting the right objectives cannot be over-emphasised. The objective will determine the make-up of the communications mix and the strategy(ies) adopted.

Push, pull and profile strategies

Push strategy

This involves 'pushing' the product into distribution channels, for example through personal selling, incentives and trade advertising. With a push strategy the manufacturer 'pushes' the product through the distribution channel to those members who will add value to the product.

Pull strategy

This involves 'pulling' the product through by encouraging end customer demand through advertising, sales promotions and in-store merchandising. In a pull strategy, communications are directed at the end-user rather than through the distribution channel.

Profile strategy

This involves communicating with the target audience and other key stakeholders to build and maintain the organisation's profile, or the profile of a new product/brand.

The Loyalty ladder is used to understand customer loyalty. The ladder suggests that customer relationships progress through a number of recognised levels from prospect, purchaser, client, supporter, advocate and partner.

Partner
Advocate
Supporter
Client
Purchaser
Prospect

Ladder of loyalty

Several writers have used a ladder concept to depict ascending levels of customer loyalty. One of the best known versions is the relationship marketing ladder of loyalty developed by Christopher *et al* (2008, p48):

Ladder of loyalty

- Prospect: someone (or a business) who (which) is believed to be a potential customer, ie could potentially be persuaded to do business with the organisation.

- Purchaser: someone (or a business) who (which) has done business once with the organisation.

- Client: someone (or a business) who (which) has done business with the organisation on a repeat basis, but may be negative or neutral towards the organisation.

- Supporter: someone (or a business) who (which) likes dealing with the organisation but only supports it passively.

- Advocate: someone (or a business) who (which) actively recommends the organisation, ie effectively does some marketing on behalf of the organisation.

- Partner: someone (or a business) who (which) has a strong independent relationship with the organisation.

This is a useful tool for marketers to attempt to understand the positioning, in relationship terms, of the target audience.

Communication form	Description
Personal selling	Allows complex products to be explained.
Trade advertising	Most industries and markets have a specific journal or newspaper.
Direct marketing	Direct mail in the B2B sector needs to be highly targeted which requires considerable research. Outbound telesales often used in routine purchases and relationship can be built through this approach. Support for the sales team by making courtesy calls again to build the relationship.
Sales promotion	Tactical way to generate increased sales by offering additional incentives on selected product lines for a short period of time.
Exhibitions	Often used to focus on an organisation's new product range where potential buyers come specifically to see the season's new range(s).
PR	PR is largely outside of the control of an organisation, however, it is an important tool and needs to be managed effectively.
Internet/online	An increasingly important medium. Web acts as showcase for the organisation and, while impersonal, offers cost savings and improved efficiencies especially when linked with e-commerce. Social media is becoming increasingly popular in both B2B and B2C marketing.

Standardisation versus adaptation of media messages

Adaptation	
	■ A central theme can be tailored to the needs of the local market making it more tailored and relevant. It can also be modified to show greater understanding of the individual market as the message can be developed by 'local people for local people'.
	■ Adapting the communication recognises that local needs do vary and a generic message may not always be appropriate. Needs, wants, purchasing habits, behaviours, and so on vary across markets.
	■ Educational levels vary and 'sophisticated' messages may not always be appropriate. Similarly, as we have seen with the concept of culture, messages can be interpreted differently.
	■ Legal issues and constraints will vary across national boundaries and sometimes within countries, so what may be acceptable in one market may not be acceptable in another and similarly different codes of practice with legal or voluntary controls may be in place.

UK legislation

- **The Data Protection Act 1984**: certain organisations must be registered with the data protection registrar if they hold data on individuals and there are conditions about how the data is to be maintained.
- **The Control of Misleading Advertising Advertisements Regulations 1988**: where complaints regarding marketing communications will be considered.
- **The Sale of Goods Act 1979**: requires that goods must match their description.
- **The Trades Description Act 1968**: organisations must not make false or misleading statements about the products (including services).
- **The Office of Fair Trading (OFT)** aims to ensure that competition and consumer protection laws are followed.
- **The Advertising Standards Authority (ASA)** oversees the British Code of Advertising, Sales Promotion and Direct Marketing which should be:
  - Legal, decent, honest and truthful
  - Responsible to consumers and society
  - In line with the principles of fair competition
- **The Data Protection Act 1998.**
  The Act defines eight data protection principles. It also requires companies and individuals to keep personal information to themselves.

Internal Communication

The overall objective of internal marketing is to improve the quality of service offered to customers. Internal marketing is shaped by the prevailing culture of the organisation as it is this culture that provides the context within which internal marketing takes place.

An internal marketing plan (derived from the overall marketing plan) is necessary to ensure the achievement of organisation goals. The key components of an internal plan could include:

- Organisation aims and objectives
- Marketing strategy
- Segmentation, targeting and positioning (STP)
- Marketing programmes (see below)
- Implementation
- Monitoring and control

Why Internal communications?

These are important for a number of reasons:

- Staff need to be kept informed about plans, objectives and other developments.
- Customer-facing staff must be kept informed about new products and relevant policy changes.
- Clear communication is important for motivation and morale.
- Support staff engagement.
- Encourage information sharing and cross-functional collaboration.
- Promote customer/marketing orientation.

The role of Internal Communications

These are important for a number of reasons:

- **Teambuilding**: ensuring that barriers between different divisions are broken down so that all staff are working towards providing customers with service excellence and reducing the potential for conflict.
- **Goal setting**: so that the focus is on achieving corporate goals which are clearly stated and measurable.
- **Involvement**: a channel needs to be created so that problems and issues can be resolved in a constructive manner.
- **Change management**: making changes to current structures and process and responding rapidly (internally) to external changes.

Hooley *et al* (2008)

Potential audiences

Can be categorised into three groups:

- **Consumers**: the purchasers of the product

- **Channel members**: wholesalers and other members of the distribution channel

- **Stakeholders**: broader interest groups with an interest in the organisation and its activities

The role of communications with the external stakeholders is to maintain relationships through on-going dialogue and through multiple points of contact. However, it is not always immediately obvious who the key stakeholders are, and therefore like other stakeholder groups, a mapping exercise needs to be undertaken to establish the key groups.

9: MarComms activities and measurement

Topic List

The communications mix

Online/social media

Integrated marketing communications

MarComms models

Evaluating effectiveness

It is important to recognise that it is the 'mixing' of the promotional tools that generate competitive advantage for an organisation both internally and externally. However, any marketing spend must be measured to ensure that not only is value for money being received, but that the objectives set are being met.

Marketing communication tools

Above-the-line

Above-the-line activity relates to paid-for promotional activities carried out through mass media.

Through-the-line

This refers to activity that involves above- and below-the-line communications where one form of advertising points the consumer to another form of advertising, thereby crossing the line.

Below-the-line

Below-the-line includes sales promotion, public relations and personal selling.

Advertising: 'paid for' and non-personal visual/audio marketing communications activity. There are many types, eg newspaper, magazine, TV, radio, cinema, outdoor and online.

Personal selling: the use of a direct sales resource (using people) through personal contact with the customer and with the purpose of making a sale.

Public relations (PR): media coverage about the organisation and/or its products, which is not paid for by the organisation and therefore cannot be controlled.

Direct marketing: marketing communications, using various media, which interact directly with the consumer, generally providing a 'call for action' from the customer, eg, to order a product or to telephone for further information.

Viral marketing: a marketing communications activity, which is specifically created to encourage the initial recipient to pass it on, generally electronically, to friends and family.

Guerrilla marketing: tactical marketing communications activities which are typically low budget and delivered on a local scale. Such activities are frequently unconventional in nature and designed to have an element of surprise in order to make the activity/brand more memorable.

Ambush marketing: effectively 'piggybacking' unofficially on another organisation's sponsorship of an event

Integrated marketing communications mix

Having looked at the different promotional tools individually, generally they will be used together (integrated) so that the key messages can be communicated in a consistent way. Each promotional tool and choice of media should be used to support each other and reinforce the key messages. If this does not happen, then the customer is likely to become confused as a result of the mixed messages and less likely to make a purchase.

AIDA

This model suggests that the communication(s) should lead the target audience sequentially through

Awareness/Interest/Desire/Action

Marketing communications activities should focus on the above, with different elements of the communications mix used at each of the stages. Marketers should, therefore, focus on developing communications which have a clear message that will create awareness and stimulate interest. Further information (or stimulants) can then be used to encourage desire, with a 'call to action' resulting in a change of opinion or closure of a sale. There will not always be a specific 'call to action' from communications activities. The action may be an increase in awareness or brand recognition. In sales campaigns the 'call to action' may be a prompt for the customer to call a telephone number or to click on a website.

DAGMAR

The DAGMAR (Defining Advertising Goals for Measured Advertising Results) model is similar to AIDA. This model is based on the premise that buyers will go through a number of stages pre-purchase decision. The stages are:

- Unawareness: this stage is pre-communications activities.

- Awareness: this stage is necessary for the target audience to understand the message from the marketing organisation.

- Comprehension: the buyer must understand the message, ie just awareness is not sufficient.

- Conviction: the buyer must progress beyond simply comprehending the message they must be convinced of its meaning.

Various promotional tools assessed against the criteria of communications, cost and control

	Advertising	Sales promotion	Public relations	Personal selling	Direct marketing
Personal message?	Low	Low	Low	High	High
Reach large audience?	High	Medium	Medium	Low	Medium
Level of interaction?	Low	Low	Low	High	High
Credible to audience?	Low	Medium	High	Medium	Medium
Absolute costs	High	Medium	Low	High	Medium
Cost per contact	Low	Medium	Low	Low	High
Wastage	High	Medium	High	High	Low
Size of investment	High	Medium	Low	High	Medium
Targets particular audiences	Medium	High	Low	Medium	High
Adapt quickly to change?	Medium	High	Low	Medium	High

10: Managing agency relationships

Topic List

Communications agencies

Agency selection considerations

Agency remuneration/structure

Managing agencies

Large organisations may choose to undertake many promotional activities internally rather than employ external agencies but, increasingly, much of the communication activity is given to an external agency. However, this in itself, brings some choices in agency selection. What type of agency is needed, how will it be selected, and which will best suit my needs?

Full service agency: an agency that deals with all aspects of the communications process, including planning, design, production and execution.

As the name may suggest, this type of agency offers the complete range of products and services which a client may need to advertise its products: research, strategic planning, creative, media planning and buying planning.

Where the agency does not have all the skills in-house, it will sub-contract some of the work to other agencies.

Other agencies

A la carte

A client may choose to select a number of agencies to carry out its communication activities. Each will be selected for its particular area of expertise such as strategic planning, media buying or creative. While this may offer the perceived advantage of specialism, it does mean that the client must take responsibility for managing and co-ordinating the various agencies and their activities

Media independents

Media independents provide specialist media services such as planning, buying and evaluation. The agency will suggest the media, the size of the advertisement and location, and they provide a report on the effectiveness of the campaign.

New media

Online brands, mobile communications, email and viral marketing are all growing areas which require a specialist approach. Equally, the integration of on- and off-line marketing will require a greater blend of skills.

Shortlist criteria for agency selection:

1. Area of expertise held by the agencies
2. Quality of existing clients (need to consider any competitive issues)
3. Reputation of principals and experience of staff
4. Agency fees and methods of charging and payment
5. In-house resources
6. Geographical cover, ie any international contacts

It is usual to visit the agency premises to see the working conditions and have the opportunity to meet staff who may not be involved in the pitch (see below).

Those agencies invited to pitch will be given a brief by the client and a set amount of time to prepare it.

Agency remuneration methods

Reward method	Explanation
Commission	Traditionally agencies were paid a commission in exchange for using a particular publication. Commission was paid at rate of 15%. However, different agencies received different levels and clients increasingly became concerned about agency objectivity when planning media schedules.
	Consequently, the fee payment method became more popular and the concept of payment by results gained popularity.
Fees	Whatever media is chosen, payment is by a set fee for a particular activity.
	Monthly fees irrespective of the work put through the agency will be paid, known as a retainer. In addition to the retainer, a fixed price will be agreed for each component of a campaign. For example, a client may agree a fixed monthly fee in addition to a menu of prices for specific activity.
Payment by results	While popular overseas, it is used selectively in the UK. Depending on the success of the campaign different payment terms will be triggered. While many would argue the merits of the approach, an agency can argue that success is hard to define and, in any event, elements of the campaign may be outside its control.

10: Managing agency relationships

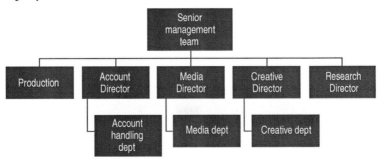

Agency structure

```
                          Senior
                        management
                           team
                             |
  ┌──────────┬──────────────┼──────────────┬──────────────┐
Production  Account        Media         Creative        Research
           Director       Director       Director        Director
              |              |              |
           Account        Media dept     Creative dept
           handling
           dept
```

The Account Director is responsible for the management of specific accounts and will have a team of Account Executives who will provide day to day support on the account dealing with routine tasks. The production team is responsible for progress, known as managing the traffic, and also for the advertisements.

Accounts team: a key role within an agency. The team comprises individuals, generally headed by the Account Director, who are responsible for managing specific client relationships.

Usually the Account Director will take responsibility for the management of an account or group of accounts depending on the complexity of the relationship. The Account Director will manage the relationship to ensure it is running smoothly and will also ensure its profitability.

Account Planner

The Account Planner has a senior role within the agency for planning the advertising.

Yeshin (2006) identifies five key roles for the Account Planner:

1. Defining the task: The planner is responsible for bringing together key information from within the agency and commissioning research if necessary in order to clearly define the task.

2. Preparing the creative brief: The planner will develop the creative brief which informs the creative process.

3. Creative development: The planner will input into all stages of the creative development and be the 'custodian' of the client's brand values.

4. Presenting to the client: The planner will join the account handlers and present the advertising concepts to the client and answer questions regarding the rationale for the approach taken.

5. Tracking performance: Once the campaign is launched the planner will monitor consumer reaction and feedback to the campaign.

Creative team: individuals within an agency who are responsible for developing the messages, imagery and soundtracks used in communications.

It is the creative team that is responsible for developing the messages, imagery and soundtrack used in the campaign. It is usual for a copywriter to work with the Art Director to develop the creative concept. This team will interpret the creative brief and turn it into advertising, or some other form of communication.

Communications brief: a formal communication from the client to the agency detailing key information to enable the agency to develop, and in some cases deliver, a communications campaign.

Managing agencies

Beltramini and Pitta (1991) suggest four benefits of effective relationships with agencies:

1. Agencies must have a genuine interest in meeting the needs of the client in order to demonstrate a commitment to maintaining a productive relationship.

2. The relationship between the parties often requires sensitive information to be shared and consequently the agency views privileged information which offers an insight in to the nature of the client which may not be ever seen by the customer.

3. Close relationships need to be maintained between the key players in the agency and the client at both the strategic and operational levels.

4. There needs to be two-way communication between the parties and the agency needs to ensure a constant flow of ideas.

Communication brief	
Objectives	▪ What objectives have been set for the campaign and how will they be measured, ie sales conversion of leads into prospects? ▪ What behavioural or attitudinal measures will be used and over what timescale? ▪ How does the activity support the overall brand promise? ▪ Does the campaign form part of a wider campaign and if so, how does it fit in?
Target audience	▪ Who is the audience?
Product	▪ Description, positioning and features ▪ Any conditions for application? ▪ Key competitors ▪ Why should people buy this product? ▪ USPs
Creative and media considerations	▪ Research undertaken on current creative work? ▪ Any media constraints?
Logistical considerations	
Budget	▪ Exactly what does the budget cover?

Creative brief	
Campaign requirement	One off, or number of adverts
The target audience	Demographics, lifestyle, product usage/attitudes
What is the advertising intended to achieve?	
The single-minded proposition	
Rationale for the proposition	
Mandatory inclusions	Eg stockists, logos, telephone/email contact
Desired brand image	Friendly, professional, modern, etc

Agency review

Reviews will generally be conducted at two levels. Firstly, the client and agency will need to meet regularly to conduct operational level reviews. These will typically include:

- A review of work in progress

- A review of live campaigns and their performance.

In addition, the client and agency will meet less frequently, possibly annually, to conduct a strategic review. This will typically include:

- A review of future plans

- A review of changes in the market

- A review of the competitive landscape

- Sharing ideas for future initiatives, eg income generation, cost efficiencies, new business acquisition.

Information for review

In order to conduct meaningful reviews, management information is vital. This must be relevant and up to date. Typical information might include:

- Spend to date
- Spend against budgets
- Performance against targets / SLAs
- Numbers of campaigns
- Sales / leads generated from campaigns
- Press coverage achieved
- Complaints received about activities
- Hits / click-throughs on websites
- Recognition / recall rates (from advertising).

11: Customer service and care

Topic List

The marketing mix for services

What constitutes service quality?

Creating competitive advantage

Customer loyalty

Managing and improving service quality

The customer service programme

This part begins with a review of the characteristics of services and how the marketing mix is used to overcome the issues and challenges faced by services marketers. We then address what actually constitutes service quality to customers through the application of SERVQUAL, a useful model for assessing the dimensions of service quality.

The figure below, adapted from Brassington and Pettitt (2006), demonstrates the difficulty of classifying some services, although it is clearer at the extremes.

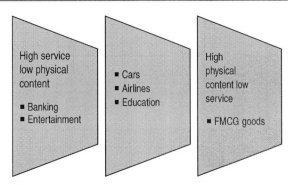

High service low physical content

- Banking
- Entertainment

- Cars
- Airlines
- Education

High physical content low service

- FMCG goods

Adapted from Brassington

The **extended marketing mix:** comprises all seven elements of the marketing mix, ie product, price, place, promotion, people, process and physical evidence.

The concept of the marketing mix (Borden, 1964) consists of four elements which when combined together create an offering for the customer. The mix known as the 4Ps (product, price, place, promotion) is not sufficient for the service sector and three additional Ps was proposed by Booms and Bitner (1981), now generally referred to as the 7Ps. The additional 3Ps are:

- **People:** take part in the production and delivery of the service and, as we will see later, may interact directly with the customer or be part of the support team

- **Processes:** the operational process that moves the customer from making the order through to taking delivery

- **Physical evidence:** the tangibility given to the product, so for example decor or brochures or the business infrastructure

Marketing services presents the marketing function with some additional challenges compared with the non-service sector, particularly around the four key characteristics of services which are

- **Intangibility/lack of ownership:** Services cannot be touched, seen, tasted, heard or smelled before being purchased, nor can they be owned. Similarly once the service has been consumed it cannot be experienced again in the same manner.

- **Inseparability:** Services cannot be stored and sold later and they cannot be separated from the provider.

- **Perishability:** As services are effectively produced and consumed at the same time they cannot be stored, so a better management of demand is necessary.

- **Heterogeneity:** The quality of the service is dependent on the person providing it, therefore it will vary.

Triangle of quality perception (Grönroos). He identified three key elements which will influence the customer's perception of service quality, ie technical, functional and customer expectations.

Triangle of quality perception

- **Technical:** Eg waiting times, such as the amount of time a customer is kept waiting on the telephone, or in a queue, or having their query dealt with. Another example is the decor in the bedroom of a hotel room.

- **Functional:** How is the measurable aspect of the service delivered? For example, was the customer advised that there would be ten-minute wait, or that the decision on a customer's loan application will take seven days?

- **Expectations:** Here the customer has their own expectation about the level of service, so the relevant factor is has the actual service lived up to their expectations?

Service satisfaction

Satisfaction is an attitude (how a customer feels about a company's product), while loyalty is behaviour (do they buy from us more than once?).

However, a 'zone of indifference' is often noted. The zone of indifference is where customer satisfaction ranges from satisfied to just satisfied. It is suggested there are two important conclusions to be drawn:

- The quality of the service provided must be outside the zone of indifference, ie it must at least make them 'very satisfied' if they are to be expected to make subsequent purchases.

- Customers must be clearly identified as to their satisfaction levels in order for the organisation to develop the appropriate actions to build enduring relationships.

Key factors in developing a competitive advantage (based on Dibb *et al*, 2005)

Key factors	Comment
Key sectors	What market sector(s) does the organisation need to develop?
Products	What product(s) need to be offered to the sectors identified? This should be based on market research.
Competitors	What advantages (perceived or otherwise) does the competition offer and what are their strengths?
Service gaps	Where are the service gaps between what the customer expects and what is delivered?
Sustainability	How can the advantage be maintained in the future?

Benefits of customer loyalty

The key benefits to be derived by an organisation when improving customer loyalty include:

- Premium pricing: existing customers tend to be content to pay a higher price than new customers.

- Cost savings: Once an organisation and the customer understand each other, the need for expensive advertising to build that part of the relationship (brand awareness) is no longer needed and more product specific (targeted) advertising can be undertaken instead.

- Income growth: as the relationship builds (ladder of loyalty), it would be expected that the customer would place additional and ongoing business with the organisation with the additional income they produce.

- Costs of acquisition: it is generally regarded five times more expensive to recruit a customer than it is to retain one, so the less need there is to recruit new customers the greater the savings. Equally, it can take a couple of years to recoup the costs of acquisition.

SERVQUAL applied to the additional 3Ps in the marketing mix

Marketing mix	SERVQUAL components
Process	■ Reliability, the ability to perform the service, accurately, dependably consistently and in accordance with the instructions given.
People	■ Responsiveness, ability to offer a timely service that meets customer expectations. When there is a problem does the organisation respond quickly? ■ Empathy, focus on the individual needs of the customer. ■ Assurance, the ability to convey trust and confidence.
Physical evidence	■ Tangibles, look and feel of offices, cars, appearance of staff and marketing collateral.

The gaps model of service (Zeithaml and Bitner, 2003)

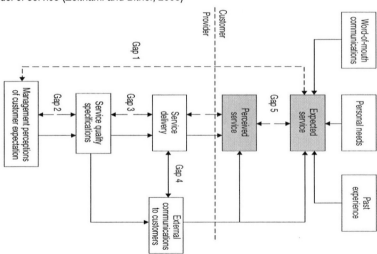

Ways of closing gaps

Gap 1	Hold regular team meetings and management briefings to ensure they are customer focused. Research in the form of customer satisfaction surveys could be undertaken to establish customer expectations and ways to exceed or delight the customers.
Gap 2	Better interaction between management and staff to establish realistic targets for staff to aspire to.
Gap 3	All customer-facing staff need to be clear on what their roles are, and what targets they are expected to achieve. Clearly internal marketing has a key role to play. It is important that staff feel valued and want to work effectively.
Gap 4	Service delivery standards need to be maintained and stronger targets set, but customers must be clear on what they can expect.
Gap 5	Clearly, if people have an expectation of what they expect, then the organisation needs to ensure the highest levels of customer service are achieved and a customer-centric approach is adopted.

Monitoring service quality

A six stage procedure is suggested:

1 **Customer service tracking studies:** The needs of customers must be clearly identified and monitored over time, so that changes can be detected at an early opportunity and action taken if necessary to address them.

2 **Quality maintenance index:** The physical service environment needs to be monitored through the use of a checklist. Key areas to be measured can include lighting, decorations, accessibility, parking and cleanliness.

3 **Mystery shopper:** A researcher poses as a customer and measures the service received against an agreed list of criteria.

4 **Staff climate monitor:** This measure looks at the customer service issue from the perspective of the member of staff and asks them where they think there are gaps.

5 **Risk point analysis:** Analysis can identify those points in the delivery of the relationship that can cause particular problems and ensure careful monitoring.

6 **Service standards review:** key information needs to be analysed and new service standards implemented, in order to match the organisation with customer needs.

(see also 12 Golden rules, in the Study Text).

12: Managing key accounts

Topic List

KAM management

The marketing mix in KAM

Managing overseas accounts

Key Account Management (KAM) is used when referring to global, national, or major corporate accounts, however as we will see below, the management of strategically important accounts overseas requires a modified approach. Often KAM is associated with an organisation's 'biggest' or 'best' customer. It has at its heart the concept that not all customers are equal and has been used in various industries such as advertising and banking for many years.

Why KAM?

Hooley *et al* (2008) suggest KAM has becoming increasingly widespread as a result of:

- Increasing levels of competition in many markets with the consequence of higher selling costs for suppliers

- Increased customer concentration as a result of mergers and acquisitions

- Growing customer emphasis on centralised strategic purchasing

- Active strategies of supplier-base reduction by larger buyers to reduce purchasing costs

Selection of Key Accounts

Below are some suggestions as a basis for selecting key accounts.

- Profitability: current and historic trends.

- Potential: what is the rate of growth and in the future?

- Annual turnover: does it meet the threshold now?

- Brand association: does the brand convey financial or non-financial benefits?

- Relationship: will the status of being a key account lead to additional business or block out the competition?

Cheverton (2008) developed a matrix that helps an organisation in an objective manner.

Key account matrix

		Low	High
Customer attractiveness	High	Key development account	Key account
	Low	Opportunistic account	Maintenance account

Relative strength

Three possible organisational approaches to KAM (based on Fill, 2006)

Approach	Summary
Assigning sales executives	This approach is warranted in smaller organisations and is very much 'hands-on'. There is a clear point of contact, roles and responsibilities are clear and there are the added benefits of flexibility and responsiveness. However, objectivity should still be maintained in this approach. Fill (2006) alerts us to the fact that this type of relationship can offer key accounts a disproportionate level of attention.
Creating a key account division	Creating a separate division can require significant structural changes, but it has the advantage of integrating the key support functions necessary in KAM. This approach is not without additional costs as many functions will be duplicated.
Creating a key account sales force	Here the decision is made to build a dedicated KAM team who can be trained to 'higher' levels so they will offer an enhanced level of service to key accounts through a solid understanding not only of the key accounts but the markets they operate in. This approach is not without its problems as once again there is duplication of work (see above).

KAM cycle (based on Millman and Wilson,1995)

Pre-KAM	At this stage there is no relationship and the task is to identify accounts that meet the selection criteria and have the potential to become key accounts. An important consideration here is to establish that the various parties could work with each other.
Early KAM	The relationship has started, but it is still transactional and there is an element of testing each other out. Communication channels will be formal.
Mid KAM	The relationship has now developed, the organisations are starting to understand each other and work proactively together.
Partnership KAM	The organisations recognise the importance of the other and first choice supplier status is achieved.
Synergistic KAM	Both organisations see themselves as one organisation where they create synergistic value in the marketplace.
Uncoupling KAM	At this stage and for a variety of reasons, the relationship is being terminated and procedures are put in place to 'wind down' the relationship.

Role of the marketing mix in KAM

Product

Products must remain relevant for key account customers, who will often be involved in helping the organisation to identify opportunities for product enhancements and developing new products.

Price

A relationship-based approach to pricing might be adopted, taking into account past and future revenue streams from the client.

Place

Flexible channels of distribution may be used, to meet the needs of the client.

Promotion

Use of the communications mix will be focused on building long-term relationships.

People

The supplier will provide the key account customer with named points of contacts, perhaps at different organisational levels.

Process

All processes must be efficient and quick. Inefficiencies are potential sources of customer dissatisfaction and should be eliminated for key account customers.

Physical evidence

Offices must look professional as should be the appearance of staff. Consistency of the brand is important, across all channels and media.

Global Account Management (GAM)

The delivery of GAM requires three competencies (Wilson *et al*, 2000):

- A forum where the customer is involved and collaborates as a part of the overall process

- Clear management of the process especially with respect to the supply of information and communication

- A co-ordinated and globally competent supply chain

13: Sales/product information & relationship risks

Topic List

Marketing information system (MIS)

Revenue generation

The customer relationship

Overcoming potential problems

Communication

An important part of any relationship is the ability of an organisation to offer customers something of value, based on previous product purchase or knowledge of the market. However, this is only possible if the organisation has detailed knowledge of its customers and the markets in which it operates.

A simple MIS which consists of three parts: external inputs, a central processing unit and outputs (adapted from Kotler *et al*, 2003)

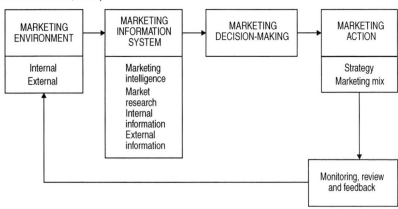

MIS

An MIS will hold large quantities of information, therefore it is essential that the quality of the data is maintained, otherwise it simply becomes a costly exercise with no beneficial output.

Each decision-maker, ie recipient of the information, will need to specify their data requirements, such as:

- Format/presentation of the information

- Data sources (external): is the information from Mintel reports, company/competitor websites, annual reports?

- Data sources (internal): key account(s), purchasing trends/patterns

- Frequency of reports: for example, weekly or daily?

The MIS will guide decisions to establish which segments of the market the organisation should target and potential income generation.

Equally, it helps in decisions about the selection of products and use of channels – particularly in regard to the potential income that may be generated.

While this source of data is largely invaluable it has to be used consistently and effectively and without being intrusive on the customer relationship. The customer wants to see the organisation making tailored offers which meet their needs rather than being treated to a demonstration of just how sophisticated the database is.

Customer Relationship Management (CRM): CRM involves the use of a database to store and disseminate important customer information to support the management of customer relationships. CRM systems can be expensive, but when effective can deliver significant value to the organisation.

The main issues CRM

- Misconceptions: there is a misunderstanding between the organisation and the customer, with the customer not receiving what they were expecting.

- Inadequate resources: caught in the desire to secure a new client or offer a competitive price, the organisation may not secure the necessary resource.

- Inadequate delivery: it is expensive to train new staff and existing staff may themselves be poorly trained leading to a disappointing service.

- Exaggerated promises: tempting for an organisation to make promises in order to secure the business but cannot deliver.

Partnership relationship life cycle

Partnership stage	Initiation stage
<ul><li>Recognition of the importance of the account to the organisation</li><li>Multiple relationship contacts at all levels</li></ul>	<ul><li>Interest generated and targets identified</li><li>Matching products to customer needs</li><li>Understanding customer needs</li></ul>
Consolidation stage	**Development stage**
<ul><li>Focus on building customer loyalty</li><li>Innovation and new product development/offering</li></ul>	<ul><li>Demonstration of organisation's ability to meet customer promises</li><li>Building resources to support the relationship</li></ul>

Overcoming potential problems

Most problems can be overcome by focusing on the needs of staff.

Staff that are motivated and happy in their work are more likely to convey positive images to the customers who in turn will be satisfied and more likely to remain as customers. Organisations can improve the service through:

Training: Service failures can often be attributed to staff who simply do not follow the existing procedures or make mistakes in carrying out a process.

Productivity: Where the levels of productivity are perceived to be below that acceptable to the organisation or the industry average, processes should be put in place to address this but the underlying cause needs to be identified.

Technology: Increasingly technology is being used to improve the customer experience.

Customer interaction: Increasingly we are moving to a team-based solution to customer needs rather than an individual one, as staff become empowered to deal with complaints.

The role of people is critical to the customer relationship, but communication is also important to the relationship, the challenge is to balance cost and frequency. The relationship between people and effective communication is fundamental to the success of the client relationship. Staff must be well trained, informed and their role valued.

Each stage of the relationship will require a different blend of the communications mix to ensure that every opportunity to maintain and build on the client relationship is taken and maximised in terms of client satisfaction and organisational profitability.

14: Analysing the case material/preparing for the exam

Topic List

The DCVTM case study

Analysing the case study

Preparing for the examination

In the examination

In this final part we consider the assessment for Delivering Customer Value through Marketing (DCVTM) and how you can prepare for it. There are three elements. First, we shall consider how to analyse the case material. Second, we shall then look at how you should prepare for the examination. Then, finally, we will consider what you need to do during the examination to enhance your chances of success.

The assessment for DCVTM) is a three-hour closed-book examination. The paper comprises three Tasks (questions). The first Task is worth 50 marks and the other two Tasks 25 marks each. All three Tasks must be completed. Some Tasks may be broken down into two or more questions. So, all questions are compulsory, ie there is no choice of questions. This, clearly, places a significant emphasis on the importance, to students, of covering every aspect of the syllabus in detail. In addition, students should note that all questions relate to the case material, which is provided to students ahead of the examination. These two aspects are important and must be duly recognised by students. As a result, all answers must also relate to the case material, ie 'generic' answers (which do not relate sufficiently to the case material) will not pass. The purpose of issuing the case material ahead of the examination is to enable students sufficient time to carry out detailed analysis of the case and so that this analysis can be applied within answers.

Cases can feature any type of organisation from any sector, or will focus on a sector itself. Some key points for students in terms of the case study:

1 The case study provides the context for the answers.

2 All the information the students need to answer the questions will be contained within the case study. So, students are advised not to waste time collecting unnecessary additional data, either about the company or the sector/market generally.

3 On no account should students contact organisations featured in the case. This is strictly forbidden.

4 Students are expected to be aware of general and topical issues which might not be specifically mentioned in the case, eg global economic issues and the impact of the recent global financial crisis.

5 Sometimes, information provided in the case study is an extract only (from more detailed sources). In compiling the case material, therefore, some anomalies may arise. Where the student identifies these they should not contact The Chartered Institute of Marketing, but should instead state clearly, within their answer, any assumptions they have made.

Ellett (2007, p26) explains that:

'The key to the process is active reading. Active reading is interrogative and purposeful. You ask questions about the case and seek answers. Questions give a purpose for reading; they direct and focus study on important aspects of a situation... Active reading is also iterative, meaning you make multiple passes through a case. With each iteration, the purpose of reading changes; you are looking for new information or looking at old information in a new way'.

A process for analysing the case study

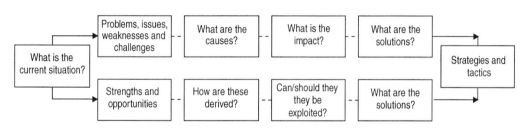

Marketing tools and models

Six markets framework	Financial analysis	Porter's five forces model
Ansoff matrix	Gaps model	Porter's generic strategies
BCG matrix	GE matrix	Pricing policy/strategy
Brand loyalty	Macro environmental analysis	Product levels
Brand onion	Market share analysis	Product life cycle analysis
Cateora's 5Cs	Marketing mix analysis	Segmentation analysis
Channel management analysis	McKinsey 7S framework	SERVQUAL
Communications strategy analysis	Mendelow power/interest matrix (stakeholder mapping)	Shell directional policy matrix
Competitor analysis	Perceptual maps (positioning)	SWOT analysis
Diffusion of innovation	PESTEL analysis	Targeting strategy

Preparing for the examination is straightforward. Students should adopt a structured approach to study, ensuring that they allow sufficient time for:

- Studying the syllabus in its entirety
- Reading more widely than just the core text (a key feature of study at this level)
- Revising ahead of the examination
- Analysing the case study material

Students should watch out for other support available. For example The Chartered Institute of Marketing occasionally runs Webinars in some subjects, which sometimes are delivered by the Senior Examiner.

Students should focus on the following in the examination:

- Answering all questions fully
- Managing time effectively. Students should spend time on each question which is proportionate to the marks available
- Presenting their answers in a carefully considered format and ensuring that handwriting is legible throughout
- Using the pre-prepared analysis to support and reinforce points. This analysis must be applied in answers and not simply referred to
- Making reference in answers to appropriate marketing tools, models and theory
- Producing answers which are strongly focused on the case material
- Ensuring that answers are complete and comments are always fully supported

- Avoiding irrelevant content
- Answering the precise question set
- Providing evidence within answers of wider reading (note that Harvard referencing is not required in the examination)
- Ensuring that the content of answers fully addresses the 'command word' used in the question. Typically, in DCVTM, questions require students to 'analyse', evaluate', 'assess', 'examine' and 'explain'. Therefore, to satisfy these answers must be detailed and points supported
- Using appropriate examples to support the points they are making
- Questions which instruct the student to 'develop a plan' require just that, ie the answer must be presented in a recognised plan format, not as an essay
- Avoid presenting answers as simple, and unsubstantiated, bullet point lists